Menta' Arithmet

UTES A DAY.

AGE 9-11

Rhona Whiteford and Jim Fitzsimmons
Illustrated by Alan Rowe

This book provides your child with twenty-eight short activities in mental arithmetic. These are designed to give regular practice throughout the last two years of Key Stage 2, and so the tasks become increasingly challenging as the child works through the book. The mathematics covered in the book reflects the work which he or she will be doing in school. Mathematical symbols (such as − and =) and language (such as **subtract** and **equals**) are explained, and a combination of the two is used. In the same way, children meet numerals (such as **2**) in some questions, and number words (such as **two**) in others.

How to help your child

- Your child should do one Practice Page at a time. It will take most children in this age band about five minutes, but younger ones may need longer. Older or more confident children may be encouraged to complete the page as quickly as possible.

- Provide a quiet place in which to work, to encourage concentration.

- Read the instructions (and the page-by-page hint provided by the lion) with your child, and make sure he or she understands the task.

- Your child will be working towards the SATs at the end of Year 6 and may need help with concentration and commitment.

- Encourage neat handwriting and presentation.

- Write the marks for the page in the box, and also on the "totaliser" on page 30. This will give your child a record of progress over time.

- Each page can be used more than once if it is completed in pencil. Scores can then be compared.

- Give positive feedback by writing a brief comment in the speech bubble at the bottom of the page. Phrases such as "Well done!", "Excellent work!" and "Good try!" will help motivate your child.

Hodder Children's Books

The only home learning programme supported by the NCPTA

Mixed questions

Find a quiet place to work. It will help you to concentrate.

1 700 + 100 = [ ] ✓

2 [ ] x 2 = 500 ✗

3 Double 45. [ ] ✓

4 Which number is one half of 80? [ ] ✓

5 Complete this sequence of numbers.

68   64   [ ]   56   [ ]   [ ] ✓   44

6 4,000 + 200 + 10 + 5 = [ ] ✓

7 Write the correct sign in the box.

65 [ ] 97 = 162 ✓

8 Write the correct sign in the box.

160 [ ] 31 = 129 ✓

9 How many months are there in 3 years? [ ] months ✓

10 Which number is one eighth of 56? [ ] ✗

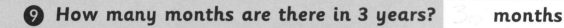

8 / 10

Mixed questions

Read each question carefully. It will help you to decide what kind of sum is needed.

① What is $1\frac{1}{2}$ metres divided by 5? 2.5 cm

② How much change did I have from £2.50 after I had spent £1.26? £ . p

③  500 ml How many jugs this size could I fill from a bowl containing 4 litres? 5 jugs

④ – ⑤ Sam had 568 straws which he put into boxes of 50.

How many boxes did he fill? 11 boxes

How many straws did Sam have left over? straws

⑥ 62 + = 100

⑦ 29 + 31 =

⑧ 63 x 10 =

⑨ Put these amounts of money in order of size. (Start with the smallest.)

£3.26   £3.62   £4.17   £2.43   £2.63

£ . p £ . p £ . p £ . p £ . p

⑩ Underline the even numbers in this row.

268   347   623   229   416   538

10

Practice Page 3

Mixed questions

Remember – a fraction is a part of a whole.

1 If $\frac{1}{5}$ of my money is 10 pence, how much money do I have? **50** p

1700   1200

2 How many hundreds are there in 1,700? **17** hundreds

3 How much heavier is 2 kilograms than 850 grams?

1150   2000g = 2 kg

4 Add 86 and 998. **1084**   **5** £5.00 x 3 = £ **15 . 00** p

6 What is 1,965 centimetres to the nearest metre? **m**

7 Write in words the time shown on this digital watch. Write your answer in analogue time.

6.50   10 to 7

8 I bought one hundred envelopes at 9 pence each. How much did I pay? £ **9.00** p

9 (81 ÷ 9) x 4 = **36**

10 Underline the fraction which has the same value as $\frac{1}{2}$.

$\frac{2}{5}$ $\frac{3}{4}$ $\frac{2}{3}$ $\frac{5}{10}$ ✓ $\frac{4}{6}$

$\frac{2}{6}$ ✗

$\frac{2}{4}$ ✓ $\frac{10}{20}$ ✓

$\frac{3}{7}$ ✗ $\frac{2.5}{5}$ ✓

$\frac{4}{8}$ ✓

/10

Doubling

Doubling means **multiplying** by 2.

Doubling large numbers is easy if you split them into hundreds, tens and units.

Double 38 → Double 30 + double 8 → 60 + 16 = 76

Try these.

1 Double 47. 94 ✓

2 Double 28. 56 ✓

3 Double 53. 106 ✓

4 Double 65. 130 ✓

This method can be used for even bigger numbers.

Double 1,232 →

Double 1,000 + double 200 + double 30 + double 2 →

2,000 + 400 + 60 + 4 = 2,464

Now try these.

5 Double 3,243. 6,486 ✓

6 Double 2,324. 4648 ✓

7 Double 4,145. 8290 ✓

8 Double 1,436. 2872 ✓

Josh has 30 pence and Harry has double that amount.

9 How much does Harry have? 60 P ✓

10 How much do they have altogether? 90 P ✓

10/10

Mixed questions

Always check your answers.

① Write in words the number shown on the abacus.

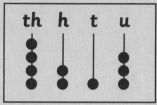

② **Which number is 100 times greater than 13?**

③ **What is the total of 58 and 41?**

④ **If four stamps cost 48 pence, how much will**
9 stamps cost? £ . p

⑤ Draw two parallel lines.

⑥ **I have 75 pence to share among five children.**
How much will each child get? p

⑦ **Two thousand plus four hundred plus seventy plus two**
equals

⑧ Round this up to the nearest kilogram: **2kg 785g** **kg**

⑨ **Find the total of 24 and 30, and subtract your answer**
from 80.

⑩ **If 8 metres of string cost 96 pence,**
1 metre will cost p

10

Practice Page 6

Mixed questions

Look at the difference between the first two numbers in a sequence. This will help you to find the other numbers.

1 Complete this sequence of numbers.

58   55   [ ]   49   [ ]   43   [ ]   37

2 How many hours are there from 8.00 a.m. to 8.00 p.m.?

[ ] hours

3 How many twenties are there in 360?   [ ] twenties

4 Add $1\frac{2}{5}$ and $\frac{3}{5}$.   [ ]

5 43 ÷ 5 = [ ]   remainder [ ]

6 Put these numbers in order of size. Start with the smallest.

3,215   1,325   2,153   1,532   1,353

[ ]   [ ]   [ ]   [ ]   [ ]

7 How much greater is £5.00 than £3.29?   £ [ ] . [ ] p

8 How many minutes are there from 9.50 p.m. to 10.42 p.m.? [ ] minutes

9 What is 254 millimetres in centimetres and millimetres?

[ ] cm   [ ] mm

10 What is $\frac{5}{8}$ of 64 pence? [ ] p

[ ]

/ 10

Practice Page 7

Mixed questions

Rounding up or rounding down numbers can help you to find the answer quickly.

1 Ten pieces of ribbon, each 25 centimetres long, are placed end to end. How long are they altogether?

| m | . | cm |

2 How much greater is 830 millilitres than half a litre? | ml

3 Add the sum of 15 and 20 to the product of 5 and 4.

4 What is the value of the 6 in this number? **3,651**

5 133 taken from a number leaves 57. What is the number?

6 Count on in tens to complete this sequence of numbers.

432   442   [   ]   [   ]   [   ]   [   ]   492

7 What is 10 metres less than 5,000 metres? [   ] m

8 How many 10 pence coins are there in £15.00?

[   ] coins

9 Round down this number to the nearest ten: **473**

10 Fill in the missing numbers on this line.

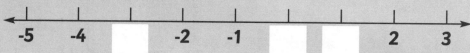

-5   -4   [   ]   -2   -1   [   ]   [   ]   2   3

10

Mixed questions

Remember – 100% is **one whole**.

① What is 50% as a fraction? ⬚

② How many more than 256 is 267? ⬚

③ 600 – ⬚ = 593

④ 26 x 3 = 78, so 78 ÷ ⬚ = 26

⑤ Share 55 pence between five children. ⬚ p

⑥ In a café, there are a hundred and twenty plates on one shelf, and fifty-six plates on another shelf.
If the waiter uses forty-three plates, how many are left on the shelves?
⬚ plates

⑦ In a class of forty children, 25% have fair hair. How many children do not have fair hair? ⬚ children

⑧ How many pence are there in £16.93? ⬚ p

⑨ Jenna spent one quarter of her birthday money on a computer game.
If she was given £60.00 for her birthday, how much did she spend? £ ⬚ . ⬚ p

⑩ Write 2,500 millilitres as litres. ⬚ l

⬚

10

Practice Page 9

Multiplying by 10, 100 and 1,000

Remember to count the noughts!

3 multiplied by **10** is **30**. You just add one nought.

3 multiplied by **100** is **300**. You just add two noughts.

3 multiplied by **1,000** is **3,000**. You just add three noughts.

Try these.

1 3 x 10 =

2 4 x 100 =

3 5 x 100 =

4 5 x 1,000 =

5 7 x 1,000 =

6 9 x 100 =

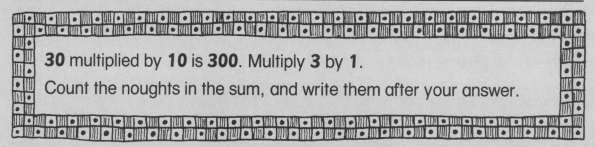

30 multiplied by **10** is **300**. Multiply **3** by **1**.

Count the noughts in the sum, and write them after your answer.

Now try these.

7 30 x 50 =

8 4 x 3,000 =

9 60 x 600 =

10 80 x 300 =

10

Practice Page 10

Mixed questions

Read the questions aloud to yourself to help you decide what kind of sum it is.

❶ Anna was eight years old in 1997.
How old will she be in the year 2007? ☐ years old

❷ I buy 2 kilograms of potatoes at 60p per $\frac{1}{2}$ kilogram.
How much change will I get from £3.00? ☐ p

❸ What is 698 to the nearest 100? ☐

❹ 75% of £1.00 = ☐ p

❺ Ten beads weigh 25 grams.
How many beads weigh $\frac{1}{2}$ kilogram? ☐ beads

❻ £8.00 – £7.25 = ☐ p

❼ $1 - \frac{2}{3}$ = ☐

❽ $\frac{3}{5}$ + ☐ = 1

❾ Write this number in words: **4,297**

☐

❿ How many centimetres are there in $\frac{3}{5}$ of 1 metre?

☐ cm

☐

10

Practice Page 11

Mixed questions

If you cannot work out the answer to a question, leave it and go on to the next one. Go back to it at the end.

1 10 x 356 = ⬚

2 Five lollipops cost 25 pence.
How much will forty lollipops cost? £ ⬚ . ⬚ p

3 I have four 50p coins, four 20p coins and three 10p coins.
How much more do I need to give me £5.00?
£ ⬚ . ⬚ p

4 What is the cost of 6 metres of tape if 1 metre
costs 80p? £ ⬚ . ⬚ p

5 Five thousand, six hundred envelopes were put into
bundles of ten.
How many bundles were there? ⬚ bundles

6 What fraction of 1 metre is 20 centimetres? ⬚

7 How many minutes is it
from 8.43 a.m. to 9.35 a.m.? ⬚ minutes

8 Josh is 113 centimetres tall.
Oliver is $1\frac{1}{2}$ metres tall.
How much taller than Josh is Oliver? ⬚ cm

9 $\frac{1}{2}$ kilogram minus 226 grams equals ⬚ g

10 A cup holds 125 millilitres of milk. How many
cupfuls will it take to fill a 1-litre container?
⬚ cupfuls

10

Mixed questions

Knowing your tables will help you with some of these questions.

❶ Complete this sequence of numbers.

159   259   ☐   ☐   ☐   659   ☐

❷ What is the square of 8? ☐

❸ (9 x 8) + 20 = ☐

❹ Which is greater, two whole ones or six quarters?

☐

❺ Underline those numbers which can be divided by 9 without leaving a remainder.

48   75   63   25   72   108

❻ 25% of a number is 16. What is the number? ☐

❼ Divide £3.84 by 6. ☐ p

❽ Double 49. ☐

❾ What is one tenth of 700? ☐

❿ Write this in numerals:

eight thousand, four hundred and thirty-seven

☐

Practice Page 13

Mixed questions

Explain how you got your answers to an adult.

① Joe was born in 1993. Oliver is six years older.

In which year was Oliver born?

② 560mm = ___ cm

③ 250ml x 8 = ___ l

④ Tom uses ten oranges to make a $\frac{1}{4}$ litre of orange juice. How many oranges will it take to make 2 litres of juice?

___ oranges

⑤ Subtract 30 from 575.

⑥ There were thirty chocolates in a box. I ate $\frac{1}{5}$ of them. How many chocolates were left? ___ chocolates

⑦ Increase £2.65 by £3.30. £ ___ . ___ p

⑧ Add $\frac{1}{4}$ of 32 to $\frac{1}{6}$ of 24. ___

⑨ 2,863 − 860 = ___

⑩ How much heavier is 1 kilogram 320 grams than $\frac{3}{4}$ kilogram? ___ g

10

Mixed questions

Time yourself. See how long it takes you to do these.

1 6 x 6 = y + 15

What is the value of **y**?

2 **What is half of £1.80?**   p

3 **What is the difference in weight between Box A and Box B?**

kg   g

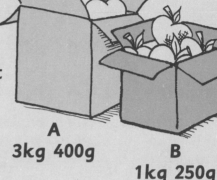

A
3kg 400g

B
1kg 250g

4 **Double 155.**

5 Write this as pounds and pence: **893p**   £   .   p

6 **How much longer than $1\frac{3}{4}$ kilometres is 1,950 metres?**

m

7 **75% of a number is 60.**
What is the number?

8 Show this time on the 24-hour digital clock:

3.25p.m.

9 **James went to the cinema at 6.45p.m.**
He left $2\frac{1}{4}$ hours later. What time did he leave?

10 **6 plus 2,000 plus 400 plus 30 equals**

10

Mixed questions

Decide that you are going to get all of these correct!

1 Ali will be 16 in the year 2004.
In which year was he born? _____

2 Add the sum of 8 and 6 to the product of 8 and 6. _____

3 A family drinks $2\frac{1}{2}$ litres of milk every day.
How many litres will they drink in 20 days? _____ l

4 Double 4,342. _____

5 Double 555. _____

6 A container holds 48 kilograms of sand.
If $\frac{3}{8}$ of the sand is used, how much is left? _____ kg

7 What is the difference between 9,000 and 900? _____

8 2,015cm = _____ m _____ cm

9 3y + 13 = 40
What is the value of **y**? _____

10 What is the cost of 9 books at 95 pence each?
£ _____ . _____ p

10

Mixed questions

Remember to check your answers.

1 What is half of 924? ▢

2 74p x ▢ = £7.40

3 What number is $\frac{3}{8}$ of 72? ▢

4 300 + ▢ = 463

5

8cm

5cm

What is the area of this rectangle? ▢ cm²

6 How much will twenty-four apples cost if four apples cost 30 pence? £ ▢ . ▢ p

7 Take away $\frac{1}{3}$ of 24 from $\frac{2}{5}$ of 100. ▢

8 Increase the sum of 15 and 30 by the product of 6 and 4.

▢

9 15 + ▢ + 23 = 57

10 Write this as millimetres:

50cm ▢ mm

▢

10

Mixed questions

If you make a mistake, find out where you went wrong!

① By how much is 3,000 metres short of 4 kilometres?

[   ] **m**

② What percentage of £1.00 is 50 pence? [   ] **%**

③ 3 + 20 + 500 + 7,000 = [   ]

④ £8.80 − £5.35 = **£** [ ] **.** [ ] **p**

⑤ 3.64 add 2.25 equals [   ]

⑥ Football stickers cost 25 pence each.
How much will I have to pay for nine? **£** [ ] **.** [ ] **p**

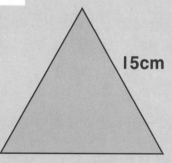

⑦ Round up £4.28 to the nearest ten pence. **£** [ ] **.** [ ] **p**

⑧ There were ninety people at a garden party.
$\frac{1}{6}$ were children, and the rest were adults.
How many adults were there? [   ] **adults**

⑨ What is the total length of the sides of
this equilateral triangle? [   ] **cm**

15cm

⑩ What is 0·5 of 90 pence? [   ] **p**

Mixed questions

Working in a quiet place will help you to concentrate.

① Draw a circle round the two fractions which have the same value.

$\frac{2}{5}$ $\frac{5}{10}$ $\frac{3}{8}$ $\frac{3}{6}$ $\frac{3}{4}$ $\frac{1}{7}$

② Write this time in words.

19.35

③ How many whole ones are equal to 32 quarters?

whole ones

④ Maria set out for a walk at 1.25p.m. and she returned at 3.15p.m. How long had she been walking?

hours   minutes

⑤ 8,670 ÷ 10 =

⑥ Ashley had £5.60 and he spent $\frac{2}{7}$ of it.
How much did he have left?   £   .   p

⑦ How many millimetres are there in 3 metres?   mm

Abbie walks 340 metres and Tom walks 410 metres.

⑧ How far do they walk altogether?   m

⑨ What fraction of a kilometre is that?   km

⑩ I think of a number and halve it.
The answer is 14.5. What is the number?

10

Mixed questions

Read the whole page before you answer any questions. Do the easiest first.

1 Complete this sequence of numbers:

4,150   4,300   [   ]   [   ]   [   ]   4,900

2 How many 250-gram packets of peas can be filled from a sack containing 6 kilograms? [   ] packets

3 Divide 108 by 9. Is there a remainder? [   ]

4 Write this time in numerals:

thirteen minutes to nine in the evening

(Remember to write **a.m.** or **p.m.**) [   ]

5 Subtract the product of 9 and 3 from the sum of 23 and 31. [   ]

6 Write this date in numerals:

5th July 1999 [   ]

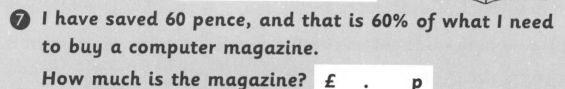

7 I have saved 60 pence, and that is 60% of what I need to buy a computer magazine.

How much is the magazine? £ [   ] . [   ] p

8 How many times larger than 150 is 1,500? [   ] times

9 $\frac{5}{6}$ of 30 kilograms is [   ] kg

10 What change do you get from £20.00 if you spend £14.89? £ [   ] . [   ] p

[   ]

10

Mixed questions

Read your work and check your answers when you have finished.

1 If a library was opened in 1942, how many years will it have been open in the year 2000? ☐ **years**

2 Put these fractions in order of size. Start with the smallest.

$\frac{7}{8}$ $\frac{2}{5}$ $\frac{6}{10}$ $\frac{2}{3}$ ☐ ☐ ☐ ☐

3 Find the sum of the odd numbers, and subtract the sum of the even numbers:

23   46   87   28   ☐

4 A car travels at 60 kilometres per hour. How far will it travel in 5 hours? ☐ **km**

5 $\frac{3}{4}l$ − 620ml = ☐ **ml**

6 40p + £2.63 + 52p = **£** ☐ **.** ☐ **p**

7 Arrange these numerals to make the largest number possible:

3   5   7   9   ☐

8 If the distance all the way around an equilateral triangle is 63 centimetres, what is the length of one side? ☐ **cm**

9 3y = 55 + 44   What is the value of **y**? ☐

10 Put in the missing sign in this sum: **(15** ☐ **4) x 5 = 95**

☐ /10

Practice Page 21

Mixed questions

How quickly can you answer these?

1 What is the value of the **8** in this number?

8,324

2 20% of a sum of money is £16.
What is the sum of money? £   .   p

3 Increase 0.63 by 0.35.

4 A bus takes half an hour to travel 30 kilometres.
If it never changes speed, how far
will it travel in 5 hours?   km

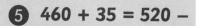

5 460 + 35 = 520 –

6 Divide the sum of 39 and 16 by 5.

7 If ten rolls of tape cost £6.60, how much does
one roll cost?   p

8 A jug contains $\frac{8}{10}$ litre of water. How many millilitres
must I add to make $1\frac{1}{2}$ litres?   ml

9 What is the smallest number that can be divided by
3 and 6 without leaving a remainder?
(The number is greater than 6.)

10 What is the product of 42 and 30?

10

Mixed questions

Remember – an even number can be divided by **2** without leaving a remainder.

① $\frac{3}{5}$ of £4.00 = £   .   p

② Which is the largest even number you can make from these numerals?

6   0   4   9

③ 12m =   mm

④ The perimeter of a rectangle is 40 centimetres. If one of the long sides measures 16 centimetres, what is the length of one of the short sides?   cm

⑤ How many 25-centimetre lengths are there in 8 metres?

    lengths

⑥ 30 tens =   fifties

⑦ 0 x 6,725 =

⑧ I have nine 50p coins, six 10p coins, eight 5p coins and ten 2p coins. How much more do I need to give me £7.50? £   .   p

⑨ 45p + 20p + 33p + 32p = £   .   p

⑩ 36 +   + 43 = 129

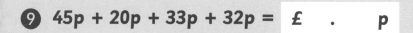

Practice Page 23

Fractions, decimals and percentages

> Start by finding $\frac{1}{10}$ of the whole number. This will help you to work out the answer.

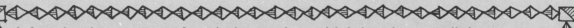

A fraction is one part of a whole number which has been split into equal parts.

One tenth ($\frac{1}{10}$) is one part of a whole number which has been split into ten equal parts.

If a whole number is split into tenths or hundredths, we can use decimals.

We can write $\frac{1}{10}$ as **0.1**.   We can write $\frac{1}{100}$ as **0.01**.

The numeral on the right of the decimal point shows how many tenths there are.

If a whole number is split into tenths or hundredths, we can use percentages.

We can write $\frac{1}{10}$ as **10%**.   We can write $\frac{1}{100}$ as **1%**.

1 Write $\frac{2}{10}$ as a decimal.

2 Write 0.3 as a fraction.

3 Write 40% as a fraction.

4 Write 60% as a decimal.

5 Write $\frac{8}{10}$ as a decimal.

Now try these.

6 $\frac{5}{10}$ of 40 =

7 0.4 of 80 =

8 30% of 90 =

9 $\frac{6}{10}$ of 70 =

10 0.6 of 50 =

10

Mixed questions

Time yourself. Work as fast as you can.

① What is one half of $5\frac{1}{2}$?

② Which number multiplied by itself equals 81?

③ In a sale, a coat was reduced by 25%.
If I paid £54.00 for it, what was the original price of the coat? £ . p

④ What must I add to the sum of 8 and 6 to make it equal to the product of 8 and 6?

⑤ What is the total of 4,250 and 3,125?

⑥ 3,254 take away 1,200 equals

⑦ How many fifths are there in eight whole ones?
fifths

⑧ What is 10% of 6 metres? cm

⑨ If six cakes cost £1.80, how much will twenty cakes cost? £ . p

⑩ What must I add to 6.4 to make 8.3?

10

Practice Page 25

Mixed questions

Explain how you got your answers to an adult.

① If the perimeter of a square is 92 millimetres, what is the length of 1 side? [   ] **mm**

② Write this number in figures:
eight thousand, six hundred and fourteen [   ]

③ Liz had eight days' holiday. If the first day of her holiday was 28th July, what was the date on the last day? [   ]

④ Round down 3 metres and 30 millimetres to the nearest metre. [   ] **m**

⑤ Oranges cost £1.36 per kilogram. How much would I pay for 250 grams? [   ] **p**

⑥ How many hours and minutes are there between 10.30 a.m. and 2.15 p.m.? [   ] **hours** [   ] **minutes**

⑦ What must I add to $\frac{1}{5}$ of 45 to make the same number as $\frac{3}{4}$ of 24? [   ]

⑧ How many whole ones equal $\frac{25}{5}$? [   ] **whole ones**

⑨ $7^2 = 38 +$ [   ]

⑩ How much of this rectangle is shaded?
Write your answer as a decimal. [   ]

[   ]

Practice Page 26

Mixed questions

To find the average of a set of numbers, find the total and then divide it by the number of members of the set.

1. 1,200 – 75 = ☐

2. Six packages of equal weight have a total weight of 8 kilograms and 400 grams.
What is the total weight of two packages? ☐ kg ☐ g

3. What percentage of 100 is 5? ☐ %

4. 360 minutes = ☐ hours

5. A bottle holds 250 millilitres of mineral water. How much mineral water would sixty bottles hold? ☐ l

6. How many seconds are there in $5\frac{1}{2}$ minutes? ☐ seconds

7. A car journey takes 3 hours and 40 minutes.
If the car arrives at 9.15 p.m., what time did the journey begin? ☐

8. Write 25% as a decimal. ☐

9. $\frac{3}{6} + \frac{5}{6} + \frac{4}{6} =$ ☐

10. What is the average of these three numbers?

21 34 11 ☐

/10

Mixed questions

Remember – the formula for area is **length x breadth**.

1 65 + 58 + ☐ = 150

2 Multiply the sum of 34 and 42 by 6. ☐

3 What is the cost of 0.5 kilograms of tea if 9 kilograms cost £162.00? £ ☐ . ☐ p

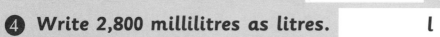

4 Write 2,800 millilitres as litres. ☐ l

5 What is the area of this rectangle? ☐ cm²

16cm

8cm

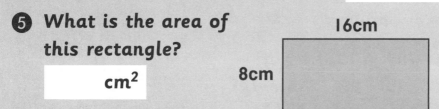

6 How many seconds are there in 0.75 minutes? ☐ seconds

7 Which three consecutive numbers come to 30 when they are added together? ☐ ☐ ☐

8 What is 75% of £12.00? £ ☐ . ☐ p

9 Trains to Manchester run every 35 minutes. If I miss the 13.10 train, what time will the next one be?
Write your answer in analogue time. ☐

10 How much change will there be from £12.00 after I have spent £4.40, £3.20 and 85 pence? £ ☐ . ☐ p

10

Mixed questions

See if you can get all these right in your shortest time so far!

1 460 + ☐ = 494

2 What is one half of $\frac{1}{5}$? ☐

3 What is the value of the first two numerals in this number?

53,246 ☐

4 Sam watches two films.
One lasts for 3 hours and 45 minutes,
and the other lasts for 2 hours and 54 minutes.

How long do they last altogether? ☐ hours ☐ minutes

5 How many days are there in 35 weeks? ☐ days

6 Increase 88 by 25%. ☐

7 Put the missing sign into this sum:

363 ☐ 48 = 315

8 What is the surface area of a cube with sides of
8 centimetres? ☐ cm^2

9 If I take 19 from a number and then divide it by 4,
my answer is 16. What is the number? ☐

10 A motorway café has 450 litres of lemonade.
One carton holds 250 millilitres.
How many cartons can be filled? ☐ cartons

Totaliser

Colour in the squares as you complete each Practice Page to show your score out of ten marks.

Practice Page

1 ☐☐☐☐☐☐☐☐☐☐   15 ☐☐☐☐☐☐☐☐☐☐

2 ☐☐☐☐☐☐☐☐☐☐   16 ☐☐☐☐☐☐☐☐☐☐

3 ☐☐☐☐☐☐☐☐☐☐   17 ☐☐☐☐☐☐☐☐☐☐

4 ☐☐☐☐☐☐☐☐☐☐   18 ☐☐☐☐☐☐☐☐☐☐

5 ☐☐☐☐☐☐☐☐☐☐   19 ☐☐☐☐☐☐☐☐☐☐

6 ☐☐☐☐☐☐☐☐☐☐   20 ☐☐☐☐☐☐☐☐☐☐

7 ☐☐☐☐☐☐☐☐☐☐   21 ☐☐☐☐☐☐☐☐☐☐

8 ☐☐☐☐☐☐☐☐☐☐   22 ☐☐☐☐☐☐☐☐☐☐

9 ☐☐☐☐☐☐☐☐☐☐   23 ☐☐☐☐☐☐☐☐☐☐

10 ☐☐☐☐☐☐☐☐☐☐   24 ☐☐☐☐☐☐☐☐☐☐

11 ☐☐☐☐☐☐☐☐☐☐   25 ☐☐☐☐☐☐☐☐☐☐

12 ☐☐☐☐☐☐☐☐☐☐   26 ☐☐☐☐☐☐☐☐☐☐

13 ☐☐☐☐☐☐☐☐☐☐   27 ☐☐☐☐☐☐☐☐☐☐

14 ☐☐☐☐☐☐☐☐☐☐   28 ☐☐☐☐☐☐☐☐☐☐

How well did you do?

Answers

PRACTICE PAGE 1
1 800   2 250
3 90   4 40
5 60 52 48   6 4,215
7 +   8 –
9 36 months   10 7

PRACTICE PAGE 2
1 30cm   2 £1.24
3 8 jugs
4 11 boxes (If a calculator is used, a decimal answer [11.36 boxes] results.)
5 18 straws   6 38
7 60   8 630
9 £2.43 £2.63 £3.26 £3.62 £4.17
10 268 416 538

PRACTICE PAGE 3
1 50p   2 17 hundreds
3 1,150g / 1.15kg
4 1,084   5 £15.00
6 20m
7 ten minutes to seven
8 £9.00   9 36
10 $\frac{5}{10}$

PRACTICE PAGE 4
1 94   2 56
3 106   4 130
5 6,486   6 4,648
7 8,290   8 2,872
9 60p   10 90p

PRACTICE PAGE 5
1 four thousand, two hundred and thirteen
2 1,300   3 99
4 £1.08
5 ═══
   The lines can be any length.
6 15p   7 2,472
8 3kg   9 26
10 12p

PRACTICE PAGE 6
1 52 46 40   2 12 hours
3 18 twenties 4 2
5 8 remainder 3
   (If a calculator is used, a decimal answer [8.6] results.)
6 1,325 1,353 1,532 2,153 3,215
7 £1.71   8 52 minutes
9 25cm 4mm   10 40p

PRACTICE PAGE 7
1 2m 50cm   2 330ml
3 55   4 600
5 190
6 452 462 472 482
7 4,990m   8 150 coins
9 470   10 -3 0 1

PRACTICE PAGE 8
1 $\frac{1}{2}$ 2 11
3 7   4 3
5 11p   6 133 plates
7 30 children
8 1,693p   9 £15.00
10 2.5l

PRACTICE PAGE 9
1 30   2 400
3 500   4 5,000
5 7,000   6 900
7 1,500   8 12,000
9 36,000   10 24,000

PRACTICE PAGE 10
1 18 years old 2 60p
3 700   4 75p
5 200 beads   6 75p
7 $\frac{1}{3}$ 8 $\frac{2}{5}$
9 four thousand, two hundred and ninety-seven
10 60cm

PRACTICE PAGE 11
1 3,560   2 £2.00
3 £1.90   4 £4.80
5 560 bundles 6 $\frac{1}{5}$
7 52 minutes   8 37cm
9 274g   10 8 cupfuls

PRACTICE PAGE 12
1 359 459 559 759
2 64   3 92
4 two whole ones
5 63 72 108
6 64   7 64p
8 98   9 70
10 8,437

PRACTICE PAGE 13
1 1987   2 56cm
3 2l   4 80 oranges
5 545
6 24 chocolates
7 £5.95   8 12
9 2,003   10 570g

PRACTICE PAGE 14
1 21   2 90p
3 2kg 150g   4 310
5 £8.93   6 200m
7 80   8 15.25
9 9.00p.m.   10 2,436

PRACTICE PAGE 15
1 1988   2 62
3 50l   4 8,684
5 1,110   6 30kg
7 8,100   8 20m 15cm
9 9   10 £8.55

PRACTICE PAGE 16
1 462   2 10
3 27   4 163
5 40cm^2 6 £1.80
7 32   8 69
9 19   10 500mm

PRACTICE PAGE 17
1 1,000m   2 50%
3 7,523   4 £3.45
5 5.89   6 £2.25
7 £4.30   8 75 adults
9 45cm   10 45p

PRACTICE PAGE 18

1 $\frac{5}{10}$ $\frac{3}{6}$ should be circled
2 twenty-five minutes to eight (p.m.)
3 8 whole ones
4 1 hour 50 minutes
5 867   6 £4.00
7 3,000mm   8 750m
9 $\frac{3}{4}$km   10 29

PRACTICE PAGE 19

1 4,450 4,600 4,750
2 24 packets   3 no
4 8.47p.m.   5 27
6 5.7.99   7 £1.00
8 10 times   9 25kg
10 £5.11

PRACTICE PAGE 20

1 58 years   2 $\frac{2}{5}$ $\frac{6}{10}$ $\frac{2}{3}$ $\frac{7}{8}$
3 36   4 300km
5 130ml   6 £3.55
7 9,753   8 21cm
9 33   10 +

PRACTICE PAGE 21

1 8,000   2 £80.00
3 0.98   4 300km
5 25   6 11
7 66p   8 700ml
9 12   10 1,260

PRACTICE PAGE 22

1 £2.40   2 9,640
3 12,000mm   4 4cm
5 32 lengths 6 6 fifties
7 0   8 £1.80
9 £1.30   10 50

PRACTICE PAGE 23

1 0.2   2 $\frac{3}{10}$
3 $\frac{2}{5}$ or $\frac{4}{10}$ 4 0.6
5 0.8   6 20
7 32   8 27
9 42   10 30

PRACTICE PAGE 24

1 $2\frac{3}{4}$ 2 9
3 £72.00   4 34
5 7,375   6 2,054
7 40 fifths   8 60cm
9 £6.00   10 1.9

PRACTICE PAGE 25

1 23mm   2 8,614
3 4th August 4 3m
5 34p
6 3 hours 45 minutes
7 9
8 5 whole ones
9 11
10 0.5

PRACTICE PAGE 26

1 1,125   2 2kg 800g
3 5%   4 6 hours
5 15l
6 330 seconds 7 5.35p.m.
8 0.25   9 2
10 22

PRACTICE PAGE 27

1 27   2 456
3 £9.00   4 2.8l
5 128cm^2 6 45 seconds
7 9 10 11   8 £9.00
9 quarter to two 10 £3.55

PRACTICE PAGE 28

1 34   2 $\frac{1}{10}$
3 53,000
4 6 hours 39 minutes
5 245 days   6 110
7 –   8 384cm^2
9 83
10 1,800 cartons

ISBN 0 340 73675 5

Text © Jim Fitzsimmons and Rhona Whiteford 1999

Illustrations © Alan Rowe 1999

The rights of Jim Fitzsimmons and Rhona Whiteford to be identified as the authors of this work have been asserted by them in accordance with the Copyright, Design and Patents Act 1988.

First published in Great Britain 1999

10 9 8 7 6 5 4 3 2 1

Published by Hodder Children's Books, a division of Hodder Headline plc, 338 Euston Road, London NW1 3BH

Printed and bound in Great Britain

A CIP record is registered by and held at the British Library.